indian
recipes
under
30
minutes

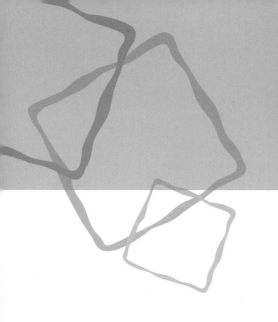

chicken lamb seafood breads

ISBN: 81-7436-350-5

© Roli & Janssen BV 2005
Published in India by Roli Books in arrangement
with Roli & Janssen BV, The Netherlands
M-75 Greater Kailash II (Market)
New Delhi 110 048, India
Ph: ++91-11-29212782, 29210886
Fax: ++91-11-29217185
E-mail: roli@vsnl.com; Website: rolibooks.com

Editor: Neeta Datta
Design: Arati Subramanyam; *Layout:* Kumar Raman
Production: Naresh Nigam, Rakesh Shrivastava

Printed and bound in Singapore

indian recipes

desserts **under** vegetarian

30

minutes

Lustre Press
Roli Books

contents

... turmeric chilli cumin coriande

cardamom **introduction** fennel...

This cookbook is unlike any other

because it teaches you the art and craft of cooking a tasty and delectable Indian meal in less than half-an-hour. The more than 70 recipes contained in it are a goldmine of instructions on not just how to create authentic flavours from all regions of India but also on how to cut down cooking time without compromising on taste. You can learn how to rustle up a delicious *degchi soola murgh* (smoked chicken) from Rajasthan; *yakhni* (stewed lamb in yoghurt) from Kashmir; *murgi kalia* (chicken in tomato curry) from Bengal; lamb stew from Kerala; *caldinho de peixe* (fish in a light coconut milk curry) from Goa; *beans nu shak* (beans cooked in Surati style) from Gujarat; and *matar ki puri* (shallow fried bread stuffed with green peas) from Rajasthan.

No more having to stuff frozen dinners, instant mixes into the microwave for people who enjoy good, fresh home-cooked food but have to make do with packaged shortcuts because their hectic schedules do not permit them to spend time in the kitchen. No more having to 'just throw a few things into a preheated oven' to prepare a quick meal for unexpected guests when you would have liked to serve something more exotic or challenging. No more having to call the nearest take-away joint or go to an expensive restaurant because home cooking is messy and tiresome. This book tells you how you can avoid taking these easy, and sometimes more costly, ways out when time is short but the palate is demanding!

For single men and women, young and old, this collection of quick and easy recipes will enable even the laziest cook to prepare a lip-smacking Indian dish in less than 30 minutes and even turn a reluctant and timid cook into an amateur chef.

basic preparations

panch phoran: Mix equal quantities of fenugreek seeds (*methi dana*), cumin (*jeera*) seeds, aniseed (*saunf*), mustard seeds (*rai*), and onion seeds (*kalonji*). Store in any airtight jar and use as and when required.

coconut milk: Grate I coconut and press through a muslin cloth to obtain the first (thick) extract. Boil the grated coconut with equal quantity of water to obtain the second (thin) extract.

If refrigerated, this can stay for up to 3-4 days.

tamarind pulp: Take 200 gm / 7 oz of seedless tamarind. Add 3 cups / 750 ml / 24 fl oz water and boil for 5 minutes. Strain the mixture and use as required.

timmur: Looks like black pepper but is sharp and pungent in taste. It is used mostly in pickles and chutneys. *Timmur* is a red seed which grows wild on thorny bushes in jungles. In India, it is found in Nainital, Mussourie, and in the hills of Himachal Pradesh. The seeds are dried and stored. Fresh seeds are more pungent in taste. Just 5-6 grains of *timmur* are sufficient to add flavour.

mangodi: Small sun-dried dumplings made from green gram (*moong*) or moth beans (*moth dal*) paste.

jimmu: It is a sort of dried grass-like ingredient, grown in Bhutan and is used only to temper dals and chutneys. It has a distinctive flavour.

lapsi: It is a roundish wild fruit with a thick skin and sour pulp. It is used in vegetables, and dals to add a sour flavour. A sweet-sour candy is also prepared from lapsi.

kachri: A sour, cucumber-like vegetable from the melon family. It is sliced and stored dried. It acts as a tenderizer for lamb dishes and provides tanginess to the dishes.

recheio spice paste: Take 10-12 Kashmiri chillies (_sookhi lal mirch_), ½ tsp cumin (_jeera_) seeds, 12 black peppercorns (_sabut kali mirch_), ½ tsp / 1 gm turmeric (_haldi_) powder, ½ small, onion, chopped (optional), ½" piece ginger (_adrak_), chopped, 12 garlic (_lasan_) cloves, 20 gm tamarind (_imli_), 1 tsp / 3 gm sugar, 1 tsp / 4 gm salt, and 6 tbsp / 90 ml / 3 fl oz vinegar (_sirka_). Grind all the ingredients to a smooth paste. Use as required.

brown onion paste: Fry sliced onions on medium heat till brown. Drain the excess oil and allow to cool. Process until pulped (using very little water, if required). Refrigerate in an airtight container.

mint chutney: Take 60 gm / 2 oz mint (_pudina_) leaves, chopped, 120 gm / 4 oz green coriander (_hara dhaniya_), chopped, 2½ tsp / 5 gm cumin (_jeera_) seeds, 2 garlic cloves, chopped, 1 green chilli, chopped, 30 gm / 1 oz raw mango, chopped, 45 gm / 1½ oz tomatoes, chopped, and salt to taste.

Blend all ingredients until paste-like. Refrigerate in an airtight container. Use as required.

chicken/lamb stock: Take 1 kg / 2.2 lb chicken / lamb bones (with some meat), 2 medium-sized onions, chopped, 1 large tomato, chopped, 4 cups / 1 lt / 32 fl oz water, 2 tsp / 8 gm salt, a pinch of turmeric (_haldi_) powder, 1" piece ginger (_adrak_), chopped, 1 tbsp / 6 gm coriander (_dhaniya_) seeds, 1 cinnamon (_dalchini_), 1" stick, 4 cloves (_laung_), and 10 black peppercorns (_sabut kali mirch_).

Put the first 6 ingredients into a large pan. Tie the ginger and spices in a muslin cloth and add to the pan. Bring the mixture to the boil, lower heat and simmer for at least 1 hour. Skim off any scum.

Squeeze the muslin bag to extract the flavours. Strain the stock. Remove the meat from the bones and keep aside. Refrigerate stock when cool and skim off any excess congealed fat, if desired.

...grill boil bake steam stir-fry

allow fry   **chicken**   deep fry

Chicken, cut into boneless cubes, washed, dried	900 gm / 2 lb
Salt	2 tsp / 8 gm
Dry fenugreek (*kasoori methi*) powder	1 tsp / ½ gm
Ginger-garlic (*adrak-lasan*) paste	2 tbsp / 36 gm / 1¼ oz
Green chillies, chopped	2 tsp
Green coriander (*hara dhaniya*), chopped	1 tbsp / 4 gm
Vinegar (*sirka*)	1 tsp / 5 ml
Vegetable oil	5 tbsp / 75 ml / 2½ fl oz
Gram flour (*besan*), sieved	5 tsp / 15 gm
Breadcrumbs, fresh	2½ tbsp / 37 gm / 1¼ oz
Egg yolks, whisked	6

murg bannu kebab

egg-coated chicken kebabs

SERVES 4-6

COOKING TIME

1. Mix salt, dry fenugreek powder, ginger-garlic paste, green chillies, green coriander, and vinegar together; rub into the chicken. Refrigerate for 15 minutes.
2. Heat the oil in a pan; stir-fry the gram flour till a pleasing smell emanates. Add chicken cubes and sauté on low heat for 3-5 minutes till half cooked.
3. Add breadcrumbs and mix well. Remove and spread on a clean table top to cool.
4. Skewer the cubes 2" apart and roast in an oven at 180°C / 350°F till done. Bring the cubes close together and coat with egg yolk. Roast till the egg coating turns golden brown. Remove, garnish with onion rings and serve hot with mint chutney (see p. 11).

1. Whisk the eggs; add cumin powder, yellow chilli powder, white pepper powder, salt, and oil. Add to the mince and mix well. Keep aside for 10 minutes.
2. Add cashew nuts, ginger, onions, green coriander, and garam masala. Mix well. Divide into 10 equal portions.
3. With wet hands, wrap two portions along each skewer. Keep 2" between each portion. Prepare 5 skewers like this.
4. Roast in a preheated oven at 150°C / 300°F for 8 minutes, basting with oil just once.
5. Remove from skewers and brush with butter.
6. Serve hot, garnished with onion rings and lemon wedges.

SERVES 4-6

COOKING TIME

murg seekh

minced chicken roasted on skewers

1 kg / 2.2 lb	Chicken, minced
2	Eggs
1 tbsp / 4½ gm	Cumin (*jeera*) powder
1 tsp / 2 gm	Yellow chilli powder
1 tsp / 2 gm	White pepper (*safed mirch*) powder
	Salt to taste
4 tsp / 20 ml	Vegetable oil
4 tbsp / 60 gm / 2 oz	Cashew nuts (*kaju*), pounded
2 tbsp / 48 gm / 1¾ oz	Ginger (*adrak*), finely chopped
4 tsp / 24 gm	Onions, chopped
5 tbsp / 20 gm	Green coriander (*hara dhaniya*), finely chopped
1 tsp / 2 gm	Garam masala
	Vegetable oil for basting
	Butter (unsalted) for brushing

SERVES 4-6

COOKING TIME

1. Marinate the chicken with yoghurt, *kachri* powder, and salt. Keep aside for 20 minutes.
2. Mix the marinated chicken with garlic paste, red chilli powder, and oil. Transfer to a pan and cook on low heat adding water, gradually, at intervals, till the chicken becomes tender.
3. Transfer to a heat-proof dish. Smoke with ghee and cloves (see p. 95) for a few minutes and then serve immediately.

degchi soola murg

smoked chicken-a Rajasthani preparation

Chicken, cut into pieces	1 kg / 2.2 lb
Yoghurt (*dahi*), beaten	1¼ cups / 250 gm / 9 oz
Kachri powder (see p. 10)	2 tbsp / 30 gm / 1 oz
Salt to taste	
Garlic (*lasan*) paste	4 tbsp / 70 gm / 2¼ oz
Red chilli powder	3 tbsp
Vegetable oil	1¼ cups / 250 ml / 8 fl oz
Water	3 tbsp / 45 ml / 1½ fl oz

600-700 gm / 22-25 oz	Chicken, skinned, cut into **8** pieces
2 tsp / 12 gm	Ginger (*adrak*) paste
2 tsp / 12 gm	Garlic (*lasan*) paste
1 cup / 200 gm / 7 oz	Ghee / Vegetable oil
	Salt to taste
1 cup / 200 gm / 7 oz	Yoghurt (*dahi*)
1 cup / 200 gm / 7 oz	Wholemilk fudge (*khoya*), liquidized
20 / 60 gm / 2 oz	Green chillies, pricked with a toothpick or fork
1½ cups / 25 gm	Mint (*pudina*) leaves, chopped
2 cups / 400 ml / 14 fl oz	Coconut milk (see p. 10)
60 / 48 gm / 1½ oz	Almonds (*badaam*), blanched, peeled, sliced, fried until light brown
90 / 48 gm / 1½ oz	Raisins (*kishmish*), soaked in water, sliced, fried for 2 minutes, drained

murg pudina

chicken á la mint

1. Marinate the chicken pieces in ginger and garlic pastes for 20 minutes.
2. Heat the ghee / oil in a pan; add the chicken pieces with the marinade and fry until lightly browned. Add the salt, yoghurt, and wholemilk fudge. Stir until the yoghurt dries up. Add the green chillies and mint leaves; stir. Pour in the coconut milk and cook on low heat until the chicken becomes tender and a thick gravy remains. Stir in the fried almonds and raisins.

SERVES 4

COOKING TIME

Chicken, skinned, cut into pieces	1 kg / 2.2 lb
Spinach (*palak*), puréed	350 gm / 12 oz
Vegetable oil	4 tbsp / 60 ml / 2 fl oz
Cinnamon (*dalchini*), 1" sticks	4
Bay leaves (*tej patta*)	2
Ginger-garlic paste	2 tbsp / 36 gm / 1¼ oz
Onion paste	1 cup / 300 gm / 11 oz
Red chilli powder	2 tsp / 4 gm
Tomatoes, chopped	180 gm / 6 oz
Maize flour (*makke ka atta*)	1 tsp
Water	2½ tbsp / 37 ml
Butter	½ cup / 100 gm / 3½ oz
Salt to taste	
White pepper (*safed mirch*) powder	1 tsp / 2 gm
Ginger (*adrak*), julienned	2 tsp / 12 gm
Fenugreek (*methi*) powder	1 tsp / ½ gm
Dry red chillies (*sookhi lal mirch*), chopped for garnishing	

saag murg
chicken in a spinach purée

SERVES 4-6

COOKING TIME

1. Heat the oil in a pan; add cinnamon sticks and bay leaves; sauté on medium heat until they begin to crackle.
2. Add ginger-garlic and onion pastes, and red chilli powder; sauté for 30-60 seconds.
3. Add tomatoes and sauté further for 1 minute. Add the spinach purée, stir in maize flour mixed with water and cook on medium heat for 10-15 minutes, stirring occasionally.
4. In another pan, heat the butter and sauté the chicken until lightly browned.
5. Transfer the chicken pieces into the spinach purée. Add salt and white pepper powder, cover and simmer on very low heat for 10-15 minutes or till chicken is cooked.
6. Serve hot, garnished with ginger, fenugreek powder, and dry red chillies.

1. Heat the butter in a thick-bottomed pan; splutter the cumin seeds. Add onions and stir-fry till brown.
2. Add the chicken mince, garlic, ginger paste, dry red chillies, salt, and tomato paste.
3. Stir-fry till the butter appears on top.
4. Add the green peas and cook till the mince and peas are cooked and the mixture is dry and golden brown in colour.
5. Remove and serve, garnished with green coriander and eggs.

SERVES 4

COOKING TIME

keema matar

minced chicken with peas

600 gm / 22 oz	Chicken, minced
250 gm / 9 oz	Green peas (*hara matar*)
2½ tbsp / 50 gm / 1¾ oz	Butter
1 tsp / 2 gm	Cumin (*jeera*) seeds
1¾ cups / 200 gm / 7 oz	Onions, chopped
2½ tbsp / 30 gm / 1 oz	Garlic (*lasan*), peeled, crushed
2 tbsp / 36 gm / 1¼ oz	Ginger (*adrak*) paste
2 tsp	Dry red chillies (*sookhi lal mirch*), crushed
	Salt to taste
3 tbsp / 45 gm / 1½ oz	Tomato paste
1 tbsp / 4 gm	Green coriander (*hara dhaniya*), chopped
2	Eggs, boiled, diced

Chicken broiler, cut into 8-10 pieces	1 kg / 2.2 lb
Yoghurt (*dahi*)	1 cup / 200 gm / 7 oz
Salt to taste	
Black cardamom (*badi elaichi*), crushed	2
Vegetable oil	4 tbsp / 60 ml / 2 fl oz
Asafoetida (*hing*)	a pinch
Bay leaves (*tej patta*)	2
Cinnamon (*dalchini*), 1" sticks	2
Cloves (*laung*)	3
Red chilli powder	1 tsp / 2 gm
Water	1 cup / 250 ml / 8 fl oz
Ginger powder (*sonth*)	1 tsp / 2 gm
Aniseed (*saunf*) powder	3 tsp / 6 gm
Garam masala	1 tsp / 2 gm

kokur roganjosh

Kashmiri chicken curry

SERVES 4-6

COOKING TIME

1. Marinate the chicken with yoghurt, salt, and black cardamom. Refrigerate for 15 minutes.
2. Heat the oil in a heavy-bottomed pot. Add the chicken, asafoetida, bay leaves, cinnamon sticks, and cloves. Cook till the yoghurt dries completely and the oil surfaces (about 10 minutes). Lower heat and cook, turning frequently, till the chicken becomes a rich brown colour.
3. Mix the red chilli powder with a few spoons of water and add to the pot. Stir briskly for a few seconds on high heat. Add 1 cup water, ginger powder, aniseed powder, and garam masala. Cook till the gravy thickens and the oil surfaces.
4. Serve hot with rice.

1. Heat the ghee in a heavy-bottomed pan; add the onions and sauté until translucent.
2. Add the ginger and garlic pastes, cloves, black cardamom, and cinnamon powder. Sauté for a few seconds or until the mixture changes colour.
3. Add the chicken and sauté for 10-12 minutes.
4. Stir in the tomatoes, coriander powder, turmeric powder, red chilli powder, and water. Cook till the chicken becomes tender and the gravy thickens.
5. Serve hot.

SERVES 4

COOKING TIME

murgi kalia

chicken in tomato curry

1	Chicken, cut into 8 pieces
¼ cup / 50 gm / 1¾ oz	Ghee
1½ cups / 180 gm / 6 oz	Onions, chopped
1 tsp / 6 gm	Ginger (*adrak*) paste
1 tsp / 6 gm	Garlic (*lasan*) paste
2	Cloves (*laung*)
2	Black cardamom (*badi elaichi*)
½ tsp / 1 gm	Cinnamon (*dalchini*) powder
200 gm / 7 oz	Tomatoes, chopped
1 tsp / 1½ gm	Coriander (*dhaniya*) powder
1 tsp / 2 gm	Turmeric (*haldi*) powder
2 tsp / 4 gm	Red chilli powder
1 cup / 250 ml / 8 fl oz	Water

SERVES 4-6

COOKING TIME

1. Heat the oil in a wok (*kadhai*); sauté the garlic paste. Add red chillies and fry for a while. Add the tomatoes and cook for 5 minutes, stirring constantly.
2. Add ginger, green chillies, and salt. Cook on medium heat for 3-5 minutes.
3. Add chicken pieces and cook till the gravy thickens and the chicken is tender.
4. Stir in red and green peppers and garam masala. Cover and cook for 3-4 minutes.
5. Garnish with green coriander and serve hot.

tomato-flavoured chicken

Chicken, cut into 12 pieces	1 kg / 2.2 lb
Vegetable oil	½ cup / 100 ml / 3½ fl oz
Garlic (*lasan*) paste	4 tsp / 24 gm
Dry red chillies (*sookhi lal mirch*), pounded coarsely	6-8
Tomatoes, blanched, chopped	1 kg / 2.2 lb
Ginger (*adrak*), chopped	2 tbsp / 48 gm / 1¾ oz
Green chillies, sliced	2
Salt to taste	
Red and green bell peppers (*Shimla mirch*)	100 gm / 3½ oz
Garam masala	1 tsp / 2 gm
Green coriander (*hara dhaniya*), chopped	1 tbsp / 4 gm

800 gm / 28 oz	Chicken thighs, boneless, cut into bite-sized pieces
5 tbsp / 75 ml / 2½ fl oz	Vegetable oil
2 tbsp / 36 gm / 1¼ oz	Garlic (*lasan*), chopped
¾ cup / 90 gm / 3 oz	Onions, sliced
1	Cinnamon (*dalchini*), 1" stick
10	Cloves (*laung*)
4	Green cardamom (*choti elaichi*)
6 tsp / 36 gm / 1¼ oz	Ginger (*adrak*) paste
6 tsp / 36 gm / 1¼ oz	Garlic (*lasan*) paste
	Salt to taste
1 tsp / 2 gm	Yellow chilli powder
2 cups / 500 ml / 16 fl oz	Chicken stock (see p. 11)
a few strands	Saffron (*kesar*), soaked in a little water for 10 minutes, crushed

murg tariwaala

chicken in thick saffron-flavoured gravy

1. Heat the oil in a saucepan; add garlic and sauté till brown. Add onions and sauté till light brown. Add cinnamon stick, cloves, and green cardamom; sauté till onions turn golden brown.
2. Add the ginger-garlic paste, chicken, salt, and yellow chilli powder. Stir for 3-4 minutes. Add chicken stock and bring to the boil. Cover and simmer till the chicken is tender.
3. Remove from heat. Take out the chicken pieces. Strain the gravy into another pot using a soup strainer.
4. Cook the gravy till it becomes sauce-like. Add the chicken pieces and cook for a minute.
5. Stir in the prepared saffron and serve hot, accompanied by any Indian bread.

SERVES 4

COOKING TIME

Eggs	8
Vegetable oil	5 tbsp / 75 ml / 2½ fl oz
Ginger-garlic (adrak-lasan) paste	1 tsp / 6 gm
Green chillies, deseeded, finely chopped	4
Tomatoes, large, skinned, deseeded	3
Green coriander (hara dhaniya), cleaned, washed, finely chopped	½ cup / 12 gm
Vinegar (sirka)	1 tbsp / 15 ml
Red chilli powder	½ tsp / 1 gm
Garam masala	½ tsp / 1 gm
Salt to taste	
Onions, sliced, deep-fried	3

lagan na tarkari per eda

egg yolks on spicy tomato mixture

SERVES 4-6

COOKING TIME

1. Heat the oil in a large heavy-bottomed pan; add ginger-garlic paste and sauté on medium heat for 2 minutes.
2. Add green chillies, tomatoes, green coriander, vinegar, red chilli powder, and garam masala. Cook till the tomatoes turn soft. Mix in the salt and fried onions.
3. Flatten the mixture evenly and make 8 depressions in the mixture. Lower heat.
4. Break each egg separately in a saucer and slip it in a depression. Repeat till all the depressions are covered with egg yolks. Sprinkle lightly with salt.
5. Cook covered till the yolks are done. Do not allow the eggs to become hard. Serve immediately.

1. Heat the ghee in a wok (*kadhai*); add onions and sauté until golden brown. Add cumin seeds, green chillies, garlic, turmeric powder, and salt; sauté for 1-2 minutes.
2. Add tomato and sauté for another minute.
3. Lightly beat the eggs and add to the above mixture. Mix thoroughly and cook for 2-3 minutes.
4. Garnish with green coriander and serve immediately on toast.

SERVES 4

COOKING TIME

akoori

spicy scrambled eggs

6	Eggs
3 tbsp / 45 gm / 1½ oz	Ghee
2	Onions, large, chopped
½ tsp / 1 gm	Cumin (*jeera*) seeds
3	Green chillies, finely chopped
2	Garlic (*lasan*) cloves, chopped
½ tsp / 1 gm	Turmeric (*haldi*) powder
	Salt to taste
1	Tomato, large, chopped
2 tbsp / 8 gm	Green coriander (*hara dhaniya*), chopped

...grill boil bake steam stir-fry

allow fry   **lamb**   deep fry

Lamb, minced	1 kg / 2.2 lb
Ginger (*adrak*) paste	3 tbsp / 54 gm / 1¾ oz
Brown onion paste (see p. 11)	1 cup / 300 gm / 11 oz
Green chillies, minced	6
Garam masala	2 tsp / 4 gm
Red chilli powder	2 tsp / 4 gm
Salt	2 tsp / 8 gm
Vegetable oil	3 tbsp / 45 ml / 1½ oz
Processed cheese	¾ cup / 90 gm / 3 oz
Onions, finely chopped	1 cup / 120 gm / 4 oz
Capsicum (*Shimla mirch*), finely chopped	100 gm / 3½ oz
Tomatoes, deseeded, finely chopped	100 gm / 3½ oz
Butter for basting	

seekh kebab gilafi

skewered lamb with capsicum, onions and tomatoes

SERVES 4-6

COOKING TIME

1. Mix the lamb mince with ginger paste, brown onion paste, green chillies, garam masala, red chilli powder, salt, oil, and processed cheese.
2. Mix together onions, capsicum, and tomatoes.
3. Squeeze out the excess water, if any, from the mince mixture and mix thoroughly. Keep aside for 20 minutes.
4. Shape the mince mixture along the length of the skewers and coat with vegetables.
5. Roast in a tandoor / oven / grill for 10-15 minutes, basting with butter at regular intervals. Remove from skewers and serve hot.

1. Mix the mince with all the other ingredients. Knead well. Let it stand for 10 minutes.
2. With wet hands, mould the mixture around the skewers pressing and shaping to about 5½"-long kebabs. Roast in a moderately hot tandoor for 12 minutes till they are browned uniformly.
3. The kebabs can also be slid off the skewers and cooked on a fine wire mesh of the grilling rack in a charcoal gas grill. Do not turn too often as they may split. Serve hot with mint chutney (see p. 11).

SERVES 4

COOKING TIME

seekh kebab

spicy minced meat skewered and roasted

500 gm / 1.1 lb	Lamb, minced
2	Black cardamom (*badi elaichi*)
2 tsp / 12 gm	Black peppercorns (*sabut kali mirch*)
½ tsp / 1 gm	Cinnamon (*dalchini*) powder
2	Cloves (*laung*)
1 tbsp / 4 gm	Coconut (*nariyal*), grated
2½ tbsp / 50 ml / 1¾ fl oz	Cream
1 tsp / 2 gm	Cumin (*jeera*) seeds
3 tsp / 18 gm	Garlic (*lasan*) paste
3 tsp / 18 gm	Ginger (*adrak*) paste
3 tbsp / 30 gm / 1 oz	Gram flour (*besan*), roasted
½ tsp / 1 gm	Mace (*javitri*) powder
1 tbsp / 15 ml	Vegetable oil
2 tbsp / 50 gm / 1¾ oz	Brown onion paste (see p. 11)
2 tsp / 4 gm	Poppy seeds (*khus khus*)
1 tbsp / 15 gm	Raw papaya paste
1 tsp / 2 gm	Red chilli powder
2 tbsp / 60 gm / 2 oz	Yoghurt (*dahi*)

Lamb, minced	500 gm / 1.1 lb
Bread slices	2
Garam masala	½ tsp / 1 gm
Onion, finely chopped	1
Green chillies, finely chopped	4
Mint (*pudina*) leaves	1 tsp
Salt to taste	
Eggs, whisked	8
Breadcrumbs	½ cup / 60 gm / 2 oz
Ghee	1¼ cups / 250 gm / 9 oz

mangsho cutlet

Bengali style lamb cutlets

SERVES 4

COOKING TIME

1. Soak the bread slices in water. Remove and squeeze out excess water.
2. Mix together the lamb mince, bread slices, garam masala, onion, green chillies, mint leaves, and salt. Keep aside for 15 minutes.
3. Divide the mixture into 10 portions; shape each portion into flat cutlets. Keep them aside on a tray.
4. Add salt to the eggs and stir.
5. Heat the ghee in a wok (*kadhai*); dip the cutlets in the egg mixture, coat with breadcrumbs and fry until golden brown. Remove and drain the excess oil; serve hot.

1. Mix together all the ingredients except the oil for frying.
2. Knead with your hands till the mixture is well blended. Divide the mixture into 15-16 equal portions. Shape each portion into flat round cutlets.
3. Heat the oil (for frying) in a pan. Shallow fry the cutlets, a few at a time, on high heat until golden brown on both sides.
4. Serve hot.

SERVES 4-6

COOKING TIME

buzith mahts

fried mince cutlets

500 gm / 1.1 lb	Lamb, minced
½ tsp / 1 gm	Red chilli powder
½ tsp / 1 gm	Ginger powder (*sonth*)
1 tsp / 2 gm	Aniseed (*saunf*) powder
½ tsp / 1 gm	Garam masala
1 tbsp / 10 gm	Gram flour (*besan*) powder, roasted (optional)
	Salt to taste
a pinch	Asafoetida (*hing*)
1	Black cardamom (*badi elaichi*) seeds
1 tbsp / 30 gm / 1 oz	Yoghurt (*dahi*)
2 tbsp / 30 ml / 1 fl oz	Vegetable oil
1 cup / 200 ml / 7 fl oz	Vegetable for frying

SERVES 4

COOKING TIME

1. Cook the lamb in a deep pot or a pressure cooker with water. Add ginger powder, aniseed powder, garam masala, asafoetida, black cardamom, 2 cloves, bay leaves, and salt. Cook for 15 minutes, or till it is almost done.
2. Add yoghurt, keep stirring till it comes to the boil. Lower heat and simmer till the gravy thickens and the lamb becomes tender. Remove from heat.
3. Heat the ghee in a small pan; add the remaining cloves and green cardamom. Sauté for a few seconds and then add to the cooked lamb. Serve, accompanied with steamed rice.

yakhni

stewed lamb in yoghurt

Lamb, washed, cut into 2" pieces	1 kg / 2.2 lb
Ginger powder (*sonth*)	2 tsp / 4 gm
Aniseed (*saunf*) powder	4 tsp / 8 gm
Garam masala	1 tsp / 2 gm
Asafoetida (*hing*)	a pinch
Black cardamom (*badi elaichi*), crushed	3
Cloves (*laung*)	4-5
Bay leaves (*tej patta*)	2-3
Salt to taste	
Yoghurt (*dahi*), whisked	2 cups / 400 gm / 14 oz
Ghee	4 tsp / 20 gm
Green cardamom (*choti elaichi*), crushed	4
Water	2 cups / 500 ml / 16 fl oz

1 kg / 2.2 lb	Lamb
1 cup / 250 ml / 8 fl oz	Water
1 tsp / 2 gm	Turmeric (*haldi*) powder
1 tsp / 2 gm	Ginger powder (*sonth*)
3 tsp / 6 gm	Aniseed (*saunf*) powder
	Salt to taste
a pinch	Asafoetida (*hing*)
2	Black cardamom (*badi elaichi*), crushed
2	Bay leaves (*tej patta*)
¼ cup / 50 ml / 1¾ fl oz	Milk
¼ tsp / 50 ml / 1¾ fl oz	Yoghurt (*dahi*)
2 tbsp / 30 ml / 1 fl oz	Vegetable oil (for tempering)
4	Cloves (*laung*)
4	Green cardamom (*choti elaichi*)

Kashmiri kalia

lamb in spicy yogurt sauce

1. Cook the lamb with water in a pot on high heat.
2. Add turmeric powder, ginger powder, aniseed powder, salt, asafoetida, black cardamom, and bay leaves. Cook, covered, for about 20 minutes on high heat. Stir occasionally.
3. Once the lamb is almost tender, cook uncovered on low heat.
4. Beat the milk and yoghurt into a smooth mixture. Add this to the lamb, stirring constantly. Bring to the boil, stirring continuously. Cook for 5 minutes more, after it comes to the boil.
5. In a small pan, heat the oil for tempering. Sauté the cloves and green cardamom for a few seconds. Add this spice mixture to the lamb. Serve with steamed rice.

SERVES 4

COOKING TIME

Lamb / Chicken, tender	1 kg / 2.2 lb
Vegetable oil	¼ cup / 50 ml / 1¾ fl oz
Cinnamon (*dalchini*), 1" sticks	3
Cloves (*laung*)	12
Green cardamom (*choti elaichi*)	4
Black peppercorns (*sabut kali mirch*), crushed	1½ tbsp
Onions, sliced long	½ cup / 60 gm / 2 oz
Green chillies, slit	6
Ginger (*adrak*), sliced long	1½ tbsp / 36 gm / 1¼ oz
Garlic (*lasan*) cloves	15
Curry leaves (*kadhi patta*)	a few
Refined flour (*maida*)	1 tbsp / 10 gm
Vinegar (*sirka*)	2¼ tbsp / 33 ml
Coconut milk, thick, extracted from 2 cups of grated coconut	½ cup / 100 ml / 3½ fl oz
Coconut milk, thin (see p. 10)	3 cups / 600 ml / 16½ fl oz
Potatoes, carrots, beans, and peas	1 cup
Black peppercorns	12

lamb stew

SERVES 2-4

COOKING TIME

1. Sauté the whole spices in oil. Add the next 5 ingredients. Sauté for a while; remove and keep aside. In the same oil, sauté the flour. Add the meat and fry slightly. Add 1½ tbsp vinegar, salt, and thin coconut milk.
2. When the meat is half cooked, add the vegetables and onion mixture. Cook covered till the gravy is reduced. Add the remaining vinegar and the thick coconut milk. Bring to the boil and remove from heat. Add the black peppercorns and serve hot.

1. Mix the minced meat with red chilli powder (1 tsp), ginger powder (¼ tsp), aniseed powder (1 tsp), asafoetida (1 pinch), yoghurt (1 tbsp), oil (2 tbsp), black cardamom seeds, Bengal gram powder, and salt. Knead well with your hand till the spices are well blended and the mixture starts to grease your hands.
2. Divide the mixture into 15 equal portions. On a flat greased surface, roll each portion gently into a 3"-long kofta. Put aside.
3. Heat the remaining oil in a deep pan. Add remaining yoghurt mixed with red chilli powder and stir briskly. When the oil separates, add the water and stir again.
4. Add the remaining ingredients and cook till the gravy comes to the boil. Carefully slide in the koftas, one at a time, and cook on high heat till the gravy starts to thicken. Lower heat and cook, stirring gently till the oil separates. Serve hot with rice.

SERVES 2-4

COOKING TIME

kofta

minced rolls in spicy curry

500 gm / 1.1 lb	Lamb, minced, without fat
1½ tsp / 3 gm	Red chilli powder
1 tsp / 2 gm	Ginger powder (*sonth*)
3 tsp / 6 gm	Aniseed (*saunf*) powder
2 pinches	Asafoetida (*hing*)
1½ tbsp / 45 gm / 1½ oz	Yoghurt (*dahi*)
6 tbsp / 90 ml / 3 fl oz	Vegetable oil
3	Black cardamom (*badi elaichi*) seeds; crushed, skins kept aside
1¼ tbsp / 30 gm / 1 oz	Bengal gram (*chana dal*), roasted, powdered
	Salt to taste
1 cup / 250 ml / 8 fl oz	Water
½ tsp / 1 gm	Garam masala
4	Cloves (*laung*)
2	Bay leaves (*tej patta*)

Liver (*kaleji*), cut into 1 cm pieces	500 gm / 1.1 lb
Vegetable oil	4 tbsp / 60 ml / 2 fl oz
Asafoetida (*hing*)	a pinch
Salt to taste	
Cloves (*laung*)	2
Red chilli powder	1 tsp / 2 gm
Water	1 cup / 250 ml / 8 fl oz
Aniseed (*saunf*) powder	2 tsp / 4 gm
Ginger powder (*sonth*)	½ tsp / 1 gm
Garam masala	½ tsp / 1 gm
Tamarind (*imli*), extract (see p. 10)	¼ cup / 50 gm / 1¾ oz
Green chillies, slit	2

tsok-tsarvan

tangy liver curry

SERVES 4-6

COOKING TIME

1. Heat the oil in a pan; add the liver, asafoetida, salt, and cloves. Sauté for 4-5 minutes on low heat.
2. Mix the red chilli powder in a little water and add to the liver. Stir briskly on high heat for a few seconds.
3. Add the remaining water, aniseed powder, ginger powder, and garam masala. Cook till the water is reduced to half.
4. Add the tamarind extract and green chillies. Cook till the oil surfaces. Remove from heat and serve with bread or rice.

1. Heat the oil in a heavy-bottomed pot; add the liver, potatoes, tomatoes, cloves, asafoetida, and salt. Cook, stirring occasionally, till the liquid dries and the oil separates.
2. Mix the red chilli powder in a little water and add to the liver. Stir for a few seconds, then add the remaining water and bring to the boil.
3. Put in the ginger powder, aniseed powder, and green chillies. Cook till the gravy thickens a little. Serve hot.

SERVES 4-6

COOKING TIME

tsarvan olu

curried liver and potatoes

500 gm / 1.1 lb	Liver (*kaleji*), cut into 1" cubes
4 tbsp / 60 ml / 2 fl oz	Vegetable oil
250 gm / 9 oz	Potatoes, peeled, cut into 1" cubes
100 gm / 3½ oz	Tomatoes, finely chopped
4	Cloves (*laung*)
a pinch	Asafoetida (*hing*)
	Salt to taste
1 tsp / 2 gm	Red chilli powder
1 cup / 250 ml / 8 fl oz	Water
1 tsp / 2 gm	Ginger powder (*sonth*)
2 tsp / 4 gm	Aniseed (*saunf*) powder
2	Green chillies

...grill boil bake steam stir-fry

fish & other
seafood

Fish fillets, washed	1 kg / 2.2 lb
Yoghurt (*dahi*)	1½ cups / 300 gm / 11 oz
Turmeric (*haldi*) powder	½ tsp / 1 gm
Ghee	¼ cup / 50 gm / 1¾ oz
Cloves (*laung*)	2
Green cardamom (*choti elaichi*)	2
Cinnamon (*dalchini*), 1" stick	1
Bay leaf (*tej patta*)	1
Black peppercorns (*sabut kali mirch*)	5
Onions, chopped	½ cup / 60 gm / 2 oz
Ginger (*adrak*) paste	3 tbsp / 54 gm / 1¾ gm
Red chilli powder	1 tsp / 2 gm
Salt to taste	
Raisins (*kishmish*)	¾ cup / 90 gm / 3 oz

doi maach

Bengali style fish with yoghurt

SERVES 4-6

COOKING TIME

1. Marinate the fillets in half the yoghurt and turmeric powder for 10 minutes.
2. Heat the ghee and sauté the fish till it is three-fourth done. Keep aside.
3. To the ghee, add cloves, green cardamom, and cinnamon stick. Sauté for a few seconds, then add onions and ginger paste. Cook till the onions brown a little.
4. Add the remaining yoghurt, red chilli powder, and enough water to cover the mixture.
5. Return the fish to the pan and then simmer for at least 15 minutes or until done.
6. Season with salt, add raisins and serve.

1. Heat the oil in a wok (*kadhai*); add the mustard seeds. When it starts spluttering, add the onions, garlic, ginger, and green chillies; sauté for a few minutes.
2. Add the ground spice paste and sardines; fry on low heat till brown. Add curry leaves, water, cocum, and salt. Bring to the boil and then simmer till the gravy thickens and the fish is cooked.
3. Serve hot.

SERVES 4

COOKING TIME

mathi pappas

sardines in thick gravy

500 gm / 1.1 lb	Sardines, sliced, gashed
	Grind to a paste:
1½ tbsp / 6¾ gm	Coriander (*dhaniya*) powder
½ tsp / 1 gm	Red chilli powder
2 pinches	Turmeric (*haldi*) powder
2 pinches	Black pepper (*kali mirch*) powder
2	Garlic (*lasan*) cloves
3 pinches	Fenugreek seeds (*methi dana*), broiled
3 tbsp / 45 ml / 1½ fl oz	Coconut (*nariyal*) oil
¼ tsp	Mustard seeds (*rai*)
½ cup / 60 gm / 2 oz	Onions, sliced
½ tsp / 1½ gm	Garlic (*lasan*), sliced
½ tsp / 3 gm	Ginger (*adrak*), sliced
3	Green chillies, split
1 sprig	Curry leaves (*kadhi patta*)
1 cup / 250 ml / 8 fl oz	Water
5-6 pieces	Cocum
	Salt to taste

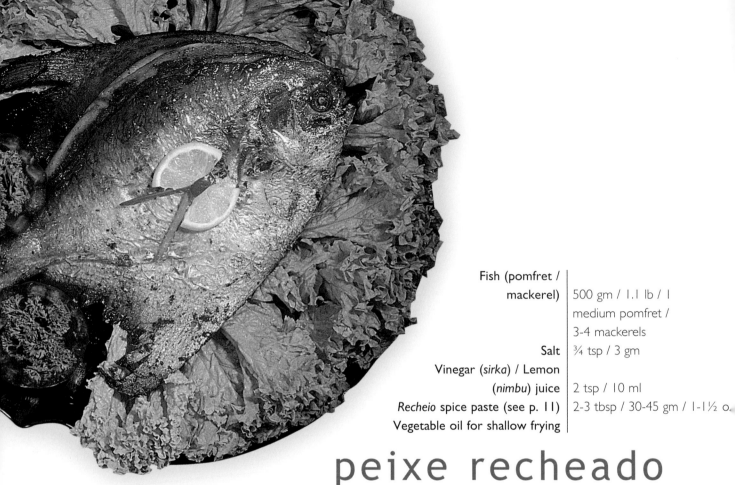

Fish (pomfret / mackerel)	500 gm / 1.1 lb / 1 medium pomfret / 3-4 mackerels
Salt	¾ tsp / 3 gm
Vinegar (*sirka*) / Lemon (*nimbu*) juice	2 tsp / 10 ml
Recheio spice paste (see p. 11)	2-3 tbsp / 30-45 gm / 1-1½ o.
Vegetable oil for shallow frying	

peixe recheado

fish stuffed with a red spice paste

SERVES 4

COOKING TIME

1. Clean the fish. Remove the internal organs and wash well. Slit the fish on either side of the bone to make 2 deep pockets. Apply salt and vinegar / lemon juice and keep aside for 10 minutes.
2. Stuff the fish with the *recheio* spice paste.
3. Heat the oil in a frying pan; gently lower the fish into the pan, and fry, uncovered, on moderate heat for 5-7 minutes on each side till golden brown. Turn the fish only once.
4. Remove from the pan and drain the excess oil on paper towels.
5. Serve hot.

1. Plunge the crabs into a pan of boiling water. Boil for a few minutes till they turn red. Drain and cool.
2. Remove the hard shells, wash and keep aside. Carefully remove and discard the stomach pouch and the gills.
3. Lift out as much meat as possible from the body. Crack the claws and remove the meat from within.
4. Heat the butter in a pan; sauté the onion till soft. Add the next 6 ingredients; and sauté for 1 minute.
5. Add the crab; cook for 2 minutes. Mix in green coriander and lemon juice. Remove from heat.
6. Mix in the egg and fill into the crab shells. Sprinkle with breadcrumbs, dot with butter and grill or bake till golden brown on top. Serve hot.

SERVES 4-6

COOKING TIME

caranguejos recheados

stuffed crabs

6	Crabs, medium-sized, washed
3 tbsp / 60 gm / 2 oz	Butter
1	Onion, large, minced
2	Green chillies, minced
1 tsp / 6 cloves	Garlic (*lasan*), minced
1 tsp / 1" piece	Ginger (*adrak*), minced
¼ tsp	Turmeric (*haldi*) powder (optional)
a pinch	Black pepper (*kali mirch*) powder
	Salt to taste
2 tsp	Green coriander (*hara dhaniya*), finely chopped
1-2 tsp / 5-10 ml	Lemon (*nimbu*) juice
1	Egg, large, beaten
¼ cup / 30 gm / 1 oz	Breadcrumbs
1 tbsp / 20 gm	Butter

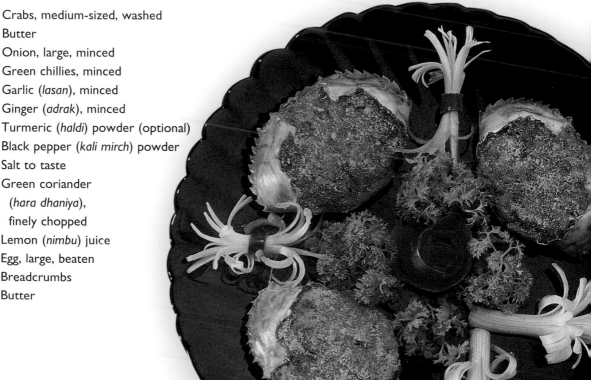

Shrimps, cleaned, deveined	50 gm / 1¾ oz
Bottle gourd (*lauki*), peeled, grated without seeds	200 gm / 7 oz
Vegetable oil	4 tsp / 20 ml
Panch phoran (see p. 10)	1 tsp / 3 gm
Bay leaf (*tej patta*)	1
Ginger (*adrak*) paste	1 tsp / 6 gm
Red chilli powder	1 tsp / 2 gm
Salt to taste	

lau chingri

shrimps with bottle gourd

SERVES 2-4

COOKING TIME

1. Heat the oil in a wok (*kadhai*); sauté the *panch phoran* and bay leaf. Add the ginger paste and cook till it browns a little.
2. Add the bottle gourd and sauté till tender.
3. Add the shrimps and sauté on high heat for a few seconds.
4. Mix in the red chilli powder and 1 cup of water. Cook on high heat till the liquid gets absorbed, stirring frequently. Serve hot.

1. Heat the oil in a broad pan; sauté the onion till light brown. Add the rice flour, sauté for 2 minutes. Add cumin powder, garlic, and green chillies; sauté for 1 minute. Add water and salt.
2. Bring the mixture to the boil. Add the fish and simmer till it is almost done. Remove the pan from the heat.
3. Mix the sugar and vinegar with the beaten eggs.
4. Pour the egg mixture into the pan and swirl it around, taking care not to break the fish.
5. Return the pan to the heat and simmer till the gravy thickens. Adjust the vinegar and sugar to get a sweet and sour taste.
6. Serve hot garnished with green coriander.

SERVES 4-6

COOKING TIME

sas ni machhi

sweet and sour fish

1 kg / 2.2 lb	Fish, fillets or cut into ½"-thick slices
2 tbsp / 30 ml / 1 fl oz	Vegetable oil
1	Onion, large, finely chopped
1 tbsp / 10 gm	Rice flour
1 tsp / 2 gm	Cumin (*jeera*), coarsely powdered
2	Garlic (*lasan*), pods, finely chopped
8	Green chillies, seeded, chopped
2 cups / 500 ml / 16 fl oz	Water
	Salt to taste
3	Eggs, beaten
1 tsp / 3 gm	Sugar
½ cup / 100 ml / 3½ fl oz	Vinegar (*sirka*)
3 tbsp / 12 gm	Green coriander (*hara dhaniya*), chopped

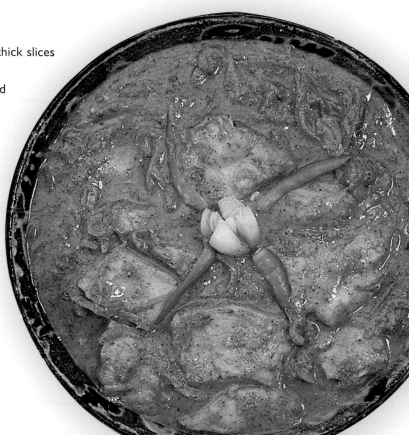

Fish	500 gm / 1.1 lb
Vegetable oil	3 tbsp / 45 ml / 1½ fl oz
Mustard seeds (*rai*)	1 tsp / 3 gm
Fenugreek seeds (*methi dana*)	a pinch
Onions, chopped	2
Ginger (*adrak*), sliced long	1½ tbsp / 36 gm / 1¼ oz
Red chilli powder, dissolved in a little water	3 tbsp
Curry leaves (*kadhi patta*)	1 sprig
Salt to taste	
Cocum, soaked in water	3 pieces
Garlic (*lasan*) cloves, chopped	12

meen vevichathu

red fish curry

SERVES 4

COOKING TIME

1. Heat the oil in a pan; add the mustard and fenugreek seeds. When they start spluttering, add the onions. Sauté for a while then add the ginger.
2. Add the red chilli water and sauté till the oil separates.
3. Add some water, curry leaves, salt, cocum, fish, and garlic. Bring to the boil. Then reduce heat and cook till the fish is tender and the gravy is thick.
4. Serve hot with rice.

1. Marinate the fish with 1 tsp each of turmeric powder and salt for 20 minutes.
2. Heat the mustard oil in a pan; fry the whole fish till three-quarters done. Remove and drain the excess oil.
3. In the same oil, add onion seeds, remaining turmeric powder, water, and green chillies; bring to the boil.
4. Add the fish and cook for about 10 minutes. Serve hot, garnished with green coriander.

SERVES 2-4

COOKING TIME

pabda maacher jhal

Bengali fish curry

250 gm / 9 oz	Fish, *pabda* or pomfret
3 tsp / 6 gm	Turmeric (*haldi*) powder
3 tsp / 12 gm	Salt
½ cup / 100 ml / 3½ fl oz	Mustard (*sarson*) oil
2 tsp / 4 gm	Onion seeds (*kalonji*)
4 cups / 1 lt / 32 fl oz	Water
5	Green chillies, slit
2 tbsp / 8 gm	Green coriander (*hara dhaniya*), chopped

Prawns, fresh	500 gm / 1.1 lb
Red chilli powder	3 tbsp
Turmeric (*haldi*) powder	1 tsp / 2 gm
Coriander (*dhaniya*) powder	¾ tbsp
Onions, sliced lengthwise	½ cup / 60 gm / 2 oz
Green chillies	6
Ginger (*adrak*), 1" piece, julienned	1
Green mango, medium-sized	1
Salt to taste	
Garlic (*lasan*)	1½ tbsp
Curry leaves (*kadhi patta*)	a few
Coconut (*nariyal*), grated	½ cup / 50 gm / 1¾ oz
Coconut oil	4 tbsp / 60 ml / 2 fl oz

chemeen manga curry

prawn and mango curry

SERVES 4

COOKING TIME

1. Mix the red chilli powder, turmeric powder, and coriander powder together. Add a little water to make a smooth paste.
2. Mix all the ingredients together except the last two in a wok (*kadhai*) and bring the mixture to the boil. Lower heat and simmer till the prawns are cooked and the gravy is thick.
3. Now mix in the grated coconut gently and pour in the coconut oil.
4. Serve hot.

1. Wash the fish, apply 1 tsp salt and keep aside.
2. Grind the coconut with ½ cup of warm water, turmeric powder, cumin seeds, coriander seeds, uncooked rice, garlic, onion, and 1 chopped green chilli to extract thick, spicy coconut milk. Grind the coconut again with 1 cup of warm water to extract thin, spicy coconut milk. Keep separate.
3. Heat the oil in a pan; add the onion and sauté for 3 minutes till soft.
4. Add the thin coconut milk, salt, and sugar; cook, partially covered for 10 minutes.
5. Add the fish and slit green chillies and cook for 5 minutes till done. Shake the pan to mix. Do not stir.
6. Add the vinegar and thick coconut milk and cook on low heat for 2 minutes, shaking the pan occasionally. Do not let the mixture boil. Adjust seasoning. Remove from heat.
7. Serve hot with steamed rice.

SERVES 4-6

COOKING TIME

caldinho de peixe

fish in a light coconut milk curry

500 gm / 1.1 lb	Fish (pomfret / *seer),* sliced
2 cups / 200 gm / 7 oz	Coconut (*nariyal*), grated
1½ cups / 375 ml / 12 fl oz	Warm water
½ tsp / 1 gm	Turmeric (*haldi*) powder
1 tsp / 2 gm	Cumin (*jeera*) seeds
1 tbsp / 6 gm	Coriander (*dhaniya*) seeds
1 tsp	Uncooked rice, washed
1 tsp / 6 cloves	Garlic (*lasan*), chopped
½	Onion, small, chopped
1 chopped + 2 slit	Green chillies
2 tbsp / 30 ml / 1 fl oz	Vegetable oil
1	Onion, medium-sized, finely sliced
	Salt to taste
¼ tsp	Sugar
1 tbsp / 15 ml	Vinegar (*sirka*)

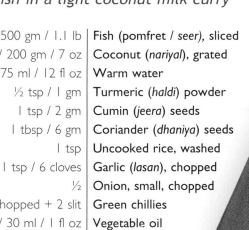

Prawns, medium-sized	500 gm / 1.1 lb
Vegetable oil	½ cup / 100 ml / 3½ fl oz
Curry leaves (*kadhi patta*)	20
Mustard seeds (*rai*)	1 tsp / 3 gm
Ginger (*adrak*) paste	2 tsp / 12 gm
Garlic (*lasan*) cloves, paste	4
Onions, chopped	½ cup / 60 gm / 2 oz
Grind to a paste:	
Dry red chillies (*sookhi lal mirch*)	4
Coriander (*dhaniya*) seeds	3 tsp / 6 gm
Turmeric (*haldi*) powder	½ tsp / 1 gm
Tomatoes, chopped	100 gm / 3½ oz
Tamarind (*imli*), extract (see p. 10)	2 tbsp / 30 gm / 1 oz
Salt to taste	
Coconut (*nariyal*), grated	½

era kozhambu

prawn curry garnished with coconut and curry leaves

SERVES 4

COOKING TIME

1. Heat the oil in a wok (*kadhai*); add curry leaves (keep aside a few for garnishing), mustard seeds, ginger-garlic paste, and onions. Sauté for a while.
2. Add the ground paste. Cook for 5 minutes. Mix in the tomatoes, tamarind pulp, and salt.
3. Stir in the prawns; after the first boil simmer for 10-12 minutes or till the prawns are cooked.
4. Heat a little oil in another pan; fry the remaining curry leaves for 3-4 seconds.
5. Serve hot, garnished with coconut and fried curry leaves.

1. Marinate the fish with salt and lemon juice; keep aside for 15 minutes.
2. Heat the sesame seed oil in a pan; sauté the onions till brown. Add the ground paste and mix well. Add the fish and simmer till tender.
3. Add vinegar, salt, sugar, and tomato purée. Mix well.
4. Serve hot with steamed rice.

SERVES 4-6

COOKING TIME

machhi patia

fish in a thick tomato gravy

750 gm / 26 oz	Fish, fillets
	Salt to taste
1	Juice of lemon (*nimbu*)
4 tbsp / 60 ml / 2 fl oz	Sesame (*til*) seed oil
8	Onions, medium-sized, grated
	Grind with a little vinegar:
6-8	Garlic (*lasan*) cloves
6-8	Dry red chillies (*sookhi lal mirch*)
2 tsp / 4 gm	Cumin (*jeera*) seeds
1 tbsp / 15 ml	Vinegar (*sirka*)
	Salt to taste
	Sugar to taste
3	Tomatoes, ripe, made into a thick purée

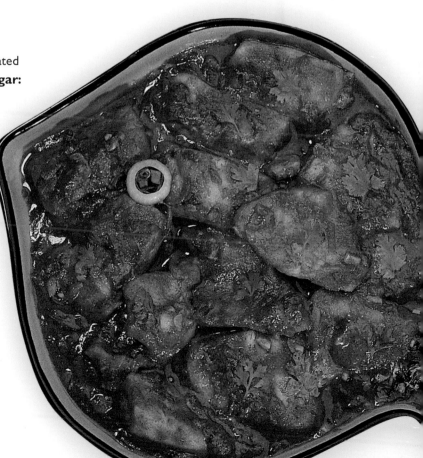

..grill boil bake steam stir-fry

allow fry **vegetarian** deep fry

Fenugreek (*methi*) leaves, fresh, chopped	1 kg / 2.2 lb
Potatoes, diced	500 gm / 1.1 lb
Ghee	4 tbsp / 60 gm / 2 oz
Dry red chillies (*sookhi lal mirch*), roasted	6
Coriander (*dhaniya*) seeds	2 tsp / 4 gm
Cumin (*jeera*) seeds	1 tsp / 2 gm
Ginger (*adrak*), julienned	2 tbsp / 36 gm / 1¼ oz
Garlic (*lasan*), julienned	2 tbsp / 36 gm / 1¼ oz
Asafoetida (*hing*)	a pinch
Salt to taste	

methi aloo

fresh fenugreek leaves with potato

SERVES 4-6

COOKING TIME

1. Sprinkle a little salt over the fenugreek leaves and keep aside for 10 minutes.
2. Heat the ghee in a wok (*kadhai*); add dry red chillies, coriander seeds, cumin seeds, ginger, garlic, asafoetida, and salt. Sauté for a few minutes.
3. Add potatoes and fenugreek leaves. Cook on low heat till the vegetables are tender and the mixture is dry.
4. Serve hot.

1. Peel the potatoes. Scoop out the centre leaving thin walls at the sides.
2. Fry the potato shells and the scoops separately. Do not let them change colour but let the sides become crisp.
3. Cool the scooped out portion of the potatoes and mash. Add salt, red chilli powder, garam masala, lemon juice, cashew nuts, raisins, and ghee.
4. Stuff the mixture into the potato cases.
5. Arrange 4 pieces on one skewer and sprinkle grated cheese on top. Grill till golden brown in colour.
6. Sprinkle with green coriander and *chaat* masala, serve hot.

tandoori aloo

potatoes stuffed with lightly spiced dry fruits

SERVES 4-6

COOKING TIME

8 / 1 kg / 2.2 lb	Potatoes, large
	Vegetable oil for frying
	Salt to taste
1 tsp / 2 gm	Red chilli powder
a pinch	Garam masala
1 tsp / 5 ml	Lemon (*nimbu*) juice
5-10	Cashew nuts (*kaju*), broken
1 tbsp / 10 gm	Raisins (*kishmish*)
2 tsp / 10 gm	Ghee
20 gm	Cheese, grated
1 tbsp / 4 gm	Green coriander (*hara dhaniya*), chopped
½ tsp / 1 gm	*Chaat* masala

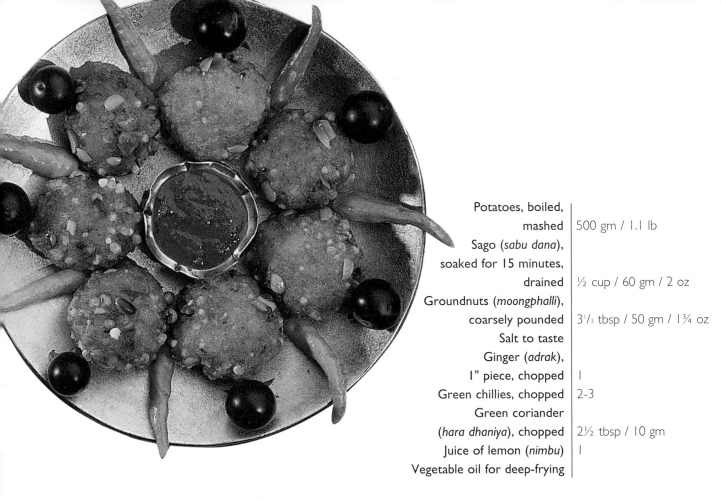

Potatoes, boiled, mashed	500 gm / 1.1 lb
Sago (*sabu dana*), soaked for 15 minutes, drained	½ cup / 60 gm / 2 oz
Groundnuts (*moongphalli*), coarsely pounded	3⅓ tbsp / 50 gm / 1¾ oz
Salt to taste	
Ginger (*adrak*), 1" piece, chopped	1
Green chillies, chopped	2-3
Green coriander (*hara dhaniya*), chopped	2½ tbsp / 10 gm
Juice of lemon (*nimbu*)	1
Vegetable oil for deep-frying	

aloo sabu dana bara

fried potato and sago cakes

SERVES 4

COOKING TIME

1. Mix all the ingredients together except the oil and divide the mixture equally into lemon-sized balls.
2. Heat the oil in a wok (*kadhai*); flatten each ball lightly between the palms and fry, a few at a time, till golden. Remove with a slotted spoon and drain the excess oil on paper towels. Repeat till all the balls are fried.
3. Serve hot with mint chutney (see p. 11).

1. In a bowl, mix together potatoes, arrowroot, salt, ginger, and red chilli powder.
2. Divide the mixture into 6 equal portions. Roll and shape each portion into flat rounds (like cutlets).
3. Heat the oil in a shallow pan. Carefully fry the cutlets a few at a time, until golden brown on both sides. Serve hot.

SERVES 4-6

COOKING TIME

olu manjivor

potato cutlets

250 gm / 9 oz	Potatoes, peeled, washed, grated
2 tbsp / 30 gm / 1 oz	Arrowroot (*araroht*)
	Salt to taste
2 tbsp / 36 gm / 1¼ oz	Ginger (*adrak*), grated
½ tsp / 1 gm	Red chilli powder (optional)
½ cup / 100 ml / 3½ fl oz	Vegetable oil

Cottage cheese (*paneer*), cut into cubes	600 gm / 22 oz
Vegetable oil	½ cup / 100 ml / 3½ fl oz
Onions, medium-sized, chopped	2
Ginger (*adrak*) paste	2 tbsp / 36 gm / 1¼ oz
Garlic (*lasan*) paste	2 tbsp / 36 gm / 1¼ oz
Red chilli powder	1 tsp / 2 gm
Coriander (*dhaniya*) powder	1 tbsp / 4½ gm
Turmeric (*haldi*) powder	½ tsp / 1 gm
Salt to taste	
Cream	½ cup / 100 ml / 3½ fl oz

malai paneer
creamy cottage cheese

SERVES 4-6

COOKING TIME

1. Heat the oil in a wok (*kadhai*). Add the onions and fry till golden brown.
2. Mix the ginger and garlic pastes, red chilli powder, coriander powder, turmeric powder, and salt together. Add to the wok and cook for 4-5 minutes.
3. Add cottage cheese cubes and stir till they are evenly coated with the spice mixture.
4. Add cream and stir well for 2 minutes or till the oil separates. Remove from heat and serve hot.

1. Combine the cottage cheese with the other ingredients, adding gram flour in the end, and mix together in a bowl to make a smooth paste.
2. Divide and shape the mixture into round croquettes / cutlets.
3. Heat the oil in a wok (*kadhai*) till it starts smoking. Slide a few cutlets / croquettes at a time into the oil and fry till golden brown and crisp on all sides.
4. Serve hot.

SERVES 4-6

COOKING TIME

paneer croquettes

cottage cheese croquettes

500 gm / 1.1 lb	Cottage cheese (*paneer*), grated
4	Green chillies, chopped
1 tbsp / 4 gm	Green coriander (*hara dhaniya*), chopped
1 tsp / 2 gm	White pepper (*safed mirch*) powder
1 tsp / 2 gm	Red chilli powder
½ tsp / 1½ gm	Carom (*ajwain*) seeds
1	Egg (optional)
1 tsp / 2 gm	Garam masala
	Vegetable oil for frying
5 tbsp / 50 gm / 1¾ oz	Gram flour (*besan*)

Split black gram (*dhuli urad dal*), soaked overnight	1 cup / 150 gm / 5 oz
Ghee	1 tbsp / 15 gm
Cumin (*jeera*) seeds	1 tsp / 2 gm
Green chillies, slit	4
Salt to taste	
Onion, sliced, fried	1
Garam masala	¼ tsp / ½ gm
Mango powder (*amchur*)	1 tsp / 2 gm
Black pepper (*kali mirch*) powder	½ tsp / 1 gm

sukhi urad dal

black gram cooked dry

SERVES 2-4

COOKING TIME

1. Rub the split black gram with your hands to remove the skin. Drain.
2. Heat the ghee in a pan; add cumin seeds and green chillies. When they start spluttering, add black gram and salt; stir-fry for 4-5 minutes.
3. Pour 2 cups of water; cook on high heat till little water remains. Lower heat and simmer till the grains are cooked and the mixture is dry. Stir gently and occasionally so that the grains don't break and stick to the bottom of the pan.
4. Transfer to a bowl; garnish with fried onion, garam masala, mango powder, and black pepper powder. A dollop of butter or 1 tbsp of hot ghee can be added to enhance the flavour.

1. Whip the yoghurt, adding enough water to obtain a pouring consistency.
2. Add the gram flour, ginger, jaggery, green coriander, curry leaves, and salt to taste.
3. Cook on high heat and stir constantly for about 15 minutes. The mixture should not be too sweet.
4. **For the tempering**, heat the oil in a pan; add the cumin seeds, fenugreek seeds, cloves, cinnamon stick, and asafoetida; sauté for a few seconds. Pour the yoghurt mixture and simmer for 2 minutes. Adjust seasoning to taste.
5. Serve hot with any vegetable.

SERVES 4-6

COOKING TIME

meethi kadhi

sweet yoghurt curry

2 cups / 400 gm / 14 oz	Yoghurt (*dahi*), sour
2 tbsp / 20 gm	Gram flour (*besan*)
1	Ginger (*adrak*), 1" piece, finely chopped
2 tbsp / 40 gm / 1¼ oz	Jaggery (*gur*)
½ cup / 12 gm	Green coriander (*hara dhaniya*), chopped
2-3 sprigs	Curry leaves (*kadhi patta*)
	Salt to taste
	For the tempering:
1 tsp / 5 ml	Vegetable oil
½ tsp / 1 gm	Cumin (*jeera*) seeds
¼ tsp / ¾ gm	Fenugreek seeds (*methi dana*)
2-3	Cloves (*laung*)
1	Cinnamon (*dalchini*), 1" stick
¼ tsp / 1 gm	Asafoetida (*hing*)

Horse gram (*kala chana*), soaked overnight	1 cup
Vegetable oil	3 tbsp / 45 ml / 1½ fl oz
Onions, sliced long	½ cup / 60 gm / 2 oz
Turmeric (*haldi*) powder	½ tsp / 1 gm
Ginger (*adrak*), chopped	¾ tbsp / 18 gm
Garlic (*lasan*) cloves, chopped	12
Green chillies	4
Cloves (*laung*)	8
Coconut (*nariyal*), thinly sliced into small pieces	¼ cup / 25 gm
Vinegar (*sirka*)	1½ tbsp / 22 ml
Salt to taste	
Curry leaves (*kadhi patta*)	a few
Coconut milk, thick, extracted from 1 cup of grated coconut (see p. 10)	½ cup / 100 ml / 3½ fl oz

kadala curry

horse gram in coconut gravy

SERVES 4-6

COOKING TIME

1. Boil the horse gram in enough water so that only ½ cup of water remains after the horse gram turns soft.
2. Heat the oil in a pan; sauté the onions, turmeric powder, ginger, garlic, green chillies, and cloves. When the oil separates, pour 1 cup of water and bring to the boil.
3. Add the cooked gram along with the water, coconut, vinegar, salt, and curry leaves. Bring to the boil.
4. Add the coconut milk and mix well. Remove from heat when the gravy thickens.

1. Snip the tips and tails of the aubergines and quarter them lengthwise. Soak in water until ready to be used, to prevent them from turning brown.
2. Heat the oil (for frying) in a broad pan. Fry the aubergines to a golden brown. Remove with a slotted spoon and keep aside.
3. Heat 3 tbsp oil in a pan. Stir in red chilli powder, mixed with 4 tsp water. Add water, fried aubergine, ginger powder, aniseed powder, asafoetida, and salt. Cook for 5 minutes on high heat.
4. Mix in the tamarind paste, add green chillies and cook till the gravy thickens and the oil separates. Serve hot.

SERVES 4

COOKING TIME

tsok vangun

tangy aubergines

500 gm / 1.1 lb	Aubergines (*baingan*), small
1 cup / 200 ml / 7 fl oz	Vegetable oil for frying
3 tbsp / 45 ml / 1½ fl oz	Vegetable oil
1 tsp / 2 gm	Red chilli powder
1 cup / 250 ml / 8 fl oz	Water
1 tsp / 2 gm	Ginger powder (*sonth*)
2 tsp / 4 gm	Aniseed (*saunf*) powder
a pinch	Asafoetida (*hing*)
	Salt to taste
4 tsp / 20 gm	Tamarind (*imli*) paste
2	Green chillies, slit

Aubergines (*baingan*), large, seedless	1 / 400 gm / 28 oz
Grind to a smooth paste with 5 tbsp vinegar:	
Kashmiri chillies (*sookhi lal mirch*)	6
Mustard seeds (*rai*)	½ tsp / 1½ gm
Cumin (*jeera*) seeds	½ tsp / 1 gm
Turmeric (*haldi*) powder	¼ tsp
Garlic (*lasan*), minced	1 tsp / 6 cloves
Ginger (*adrak*), minced	2 tsp / 2" piece
Vegetable oil	3 tbsp / 45 ml / 1½ fl oz
Garlic, chopped	1 tsp / 6 cloves
Green chillies, chopped	1-2
Granulated sugar	2 tsp / 6 gm
Salt	1½ tsp / 6 gm
Vinegar (*sirka*)	4 tbsp / 60 ml / 2 fl oz

beringelas picantes

spicy aubergines

SERVES 4-6

COOKING TIME

1. Wash the aubergines and wipe dry. Chop into 1½" cubes. Do not soak in water or wash after cutting.
2. Heat the oil in a pan; sauté the garlic and green chillies for 30 seconds. Add the ground spice paste and sauté for 2 minutes.
3. Add the aubergines and mix well. Add the sugar, salt, and vinegar. Stir well. Cover the pan with a deep metal lid. Pour a little water on the lid and cook on low heat till soft. Taste and adjust seasoning. Remove from heat.
4. Serve hot as an accompaniment to rice and curry.

1. Roast the gram flour in a wok (*kadhai*) for 5 minutes till it emanates a roasted fragrance.
2. Add all the dry spices along with water and cook till a thick paste-like consistency is obtained. Stir continuously. Remove from heat and keep aside to cool.
3. Stuff the green chillies with the gram flour paste.
4. Heat the oil and fry the green chillies, uncovered, on low heat till they become tender and change colour. Remove from heat and serve hot.

SERVES 2-4

COOKING TIME

besan ki hari mirch

green chillies stuffed with gram flour

500 gm / 1.1 lb	Green chillies, large, slit
½ cup / 50 gm / 1¾ oz	Gram flour (*besan*)
	Salt to taste
½ tsp / 1 gm	Red chilli powder
¼ tsp	Turmeric (*haldi*) powder
½ tsp / ¾ gm	Coriander (*dhaniya*) powder
1 tsp / 2 gm	Mango powder (*amchur*)
4 tbsp / 60 ml / 2 fl oz	Water
½ cup / 100 ml / 3½ fl oz	Vegetable oil

French beans, finely chopped	250 gm / 9 oz
Vegetable oil	2 tsp / 10 ml
Water	1 cup / 250 ml / 8 fl oz
Asafoetida (*hing*)	a pinch
Carom (*ajwain*) seeds	¼ tsp
Sugar	½ tsp / 1½ gm
or	
Jaggery (*gur*)	1½ tsp / 15 gm
Green chillies, slit lengthwise	2
Green coriander (*hara dhaniya*), chopped	½ tbsp / 2 gm

beans nu shak

beans cooked in Surati style

SERVES 2-4

COOKING TIME

1. Add 1 tsp oil in the water. Keep aside.
2. Heat the remaining oil in a pan; add asafoetida and sauté for a few seconds. Add the French beans, water-oil mixture, and carom seeds. Cook uncovered, on medium heat, for about 5 minutes or till the beans are tender.
3. Add sugar or jaggery, green chillies, and green coriander. Mix and serve hot.

1. Heat the oil, preferably in an iron pan.
2. When smoking hot, lower heat and add carom seeds and dry red chillies.
3. Drain the water from the spinach leaves and add to the iron pan.
4. Add salt and toss well. Cook for 4-5 minutes.
5. Remove from heat and serve.

SERVES 2-4

COOKING TIME

palunga ko saag

lightly spiced spinach

500 gm / 1.1 lb	Spinach (*palak*), washed
2 tbsp / 30 ml / 1 fl oz	Mustard (*sarson*) oil
½ tsp / 1½ gm	Carom (*ajwain*) seeds
2-3	Dry red chillies (*sookhi lal chillies*), halved
	Salt to taste

Mushrooms, halved	500 gm / 1.1 lb
Mustard (*sarson*) oil	4 tbsp / 60 ml / 2 fl oz
Asafoetida (*hing*)	a pinch
Fenugreek seeds (*methi dana*)	½ tsp / 1½ gm
Jimmu, optional (see p. 10)	½ tsp / 3 gm
Garlic (*lasan*), peeled, crushed	2 tsp / 12 gm
Onion, medium-sized, thinly sliced	1
Turmeric (*haldi*) powder	½ tsp / 1 gm
Salt to taste	
Yoghurt (*dahi*)	½ cup / 100 gm / 3½ oz
Timmur, ground (see p. 10)	½ tsp / 1½ gm
Coriander (*dhaniya*) powder	1 tsp / 1½ gm
Cumin (*jeera*) powder	½ tsp / 1½ gm
Red chilli powder	1 tsp / 2 gm
Ginger (*adrak*) paste	1 tsp / 6 gm
Tomatoes, medium-sized, chopped	2
Green coriander (*hara dhaniya*), chopped	1 tbsp / 4 gm

chiayou

tangy mushrooms

SERVES 2-4

COOKING TIME

1. Heat the oil till it starts smoking. Lower heat and add asafoetida, fenugreek seeds, and *jimmu*. Add garlic and cook till brown. Add onion and cook further till brown.
2. Add the mushrooms and cook on high heat for a minute. Mix in the turmeric powder, salt, yoghurt, all the powdered ingredients, and ginger paste.
3. When the liquid gets absorbed, add the tomatoes and cook on medium heat till the oil separates. Garnish with green coriander and serve.

1. Heat the oil in a pan; add the fenugreek seeds. When it starts spluttering, add pumpkin, salt, and turmeric powder; cook till the mixture becomes dry.
2. Add garlic, ginger, and green chillies with 2 tbsp water and mix well.
3. Mix in the *lapsi* and cook for 10 minutes more till the pumpkin gets mashed and the *lapsi* cooked.
4. Now add the dry spices; sprinkle 2 tbsp water and cook till the mixture looks pulpy.

SERVES 2-4

COOKING TIME

amilo pharshi

pumpkin cooked in mustard oil

500 gm / 1.1 lb	Red pumpkin (*lal kaddu*), peeled, sliced
3 tbsp / 45 ml / 1½ fl oz	Mustard (*sarson*) oil
1 tsp / 3 gm	Fenugreek seeds (*methi dana*)
	Salt to taste
½ tsp / 1½ gm	Turmeric (*haldi*) powder
6-7	Garlic (*lasan*) cloves, crushed
1 tsp / 6 gm	Ginger (*adrak*), scraped, ground
4	Green chillies, quartered, deseeded
6	*Lapsi* (see p. 10)
1 tsp / 2 gm	Cumin (*jeera*) seeds, dry roasted
2 tsp / 4 gm	Coriander (*dhaniya*) seeds, dry roasted, powdered

..grill boil bake steam stir-fry

allow fry **accompaniments** deep fry

Cooked rice	3 cups
Vegetable oil	3 tbsp / 45 ml / 1½ fl oz
Cumin (*jeera*) seeds	½ tsp / 1 gm
Cloves (*laung*)	3
Red chilli powder	½ tsp / 1 gm
Water	3 tbsp / 45 ml / 1½ fl oz
Salt to taste	
Ginger powder (*sonth*)	½ tsp / 1 gm
Eggs, fried (optional)	4

tud-tud bhata

fried rice

SERVES 2-4

COOKING TIME

1. Heat the oil in a deep pan; add cumin seeds and cloves; sauté for a few seconds.
2. Mix red chilli powder in a few spoons of water and add to the pan. Stir, and then quickly add the cooked rice.
3. Mix in salt and ginger powder and cook on low heat. When the rice is heated through, transfer to a serving dish.
4. Garnish the rice with fried eggs (optional) and serve hot.

1. Heat the ghee in a heavy-bottomed pot; add cloves, black and green cardamom, cinnamon sticks, bay leaves, and almonds. Stir for a few seconds, then add the mushrooms.
2. Add asafoetida and salt; sauté for a minute, and then add the rice (drained). Stir gently, add 3 cups of water and bring to the boil. Add ginger powder.
3. Mix the saffron in 2 tsp of hot water and crush with a spoon. Add to the rice mixture, cook covered for 15 minutes.
4. When the water is almost absorbed, transfer the pot over an electric hot plate or a griddle (*tawa*) and cook covered on low heat till the rice is done. Sprinkle garam masala before serving.

SERVES 2-4

COOKING TIME

kanguchhi pulao

mushroom pulao

1½ cups / 300 gm / 11 oz	Rice, washed, soaked in water
100 gm / 3½ oz	Black mushrooms (*guchhi*), washed, slit lengthwise
5 tbsp / 75 gm / 2½ oz	Ghee
6	Cloves (*laung*)
4	Black cardamom (*badi elaichi*), crushed
6	Green cardamom (*choti elaichi*)
3	Cinnamon (*dalchini*), 1" sticks
3	Bay leaves (*tej patta*)
5 tbsp / 75 gm / 2½ oz	Almonds (*badaam*), blanched
a pinch	Asafoetida (*hing*)
	Salt to taste
3 cups / 750 ml / 24 fl oz	Water
1 tsp / 2 gm	Ginger powder (*sonth*)
2 pinches	Saffron (*kesar*)
1 tsp / 2 gm	Garam masala

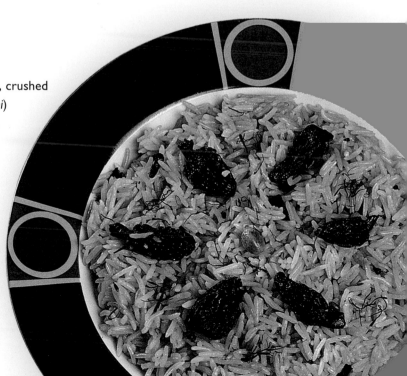

Rice, Basmati, washed, soaked for 10 minutes	½ cup / 100 gm / 3½ oz
Water	2 cups / 500 / 16 fl oz
Salt	1 tsp / 4 gm
Vegetable oil / Ghee	3 tbsp / 45 ml / 1¼ fl oz
Cashew nuts (*kaju*), chopped	½ cup / 60 gm / 2 oz
Black gram, split (*dhuli urad dal*)	½ tbsp
Mustard seeds (*rai*)	1 tsp / 3 gm
Dry red chillies (*sookhi lal mirch*)	2-3
Turmeric (*haldi*) powder	½ tsp / 1 gm
Lemon (*nimbu*) juice	6 tbsp / 90 ml / 3 fl oz
Green coriander (*hara dhaniya*), coarsely chopped	3 tbsp / 12 gm
Coconut (*nariyal*), fresh, shredded	6 tbsp / 24 gm

nimbu bhat

lemon rice

SERVES 2-4

COOKING TIME

1. Boil the water in a heavy-bottomed pan. Stir in the drained rice, salt, and ½ tbsp oil. Cover tightly, reduce heat and simmer without stirring until the rice is fluffy and tender and the water is fully absorbed. Keep aside.
2. Heat the remaining oil in a small pan. Stir-fry the cashew nuts until golden brown. Spoon cashew nuts over the cooked rice and replace cover.
3. Increase heat slightly. Sauté the split black gram and mustard seeds in the same oil. Add dry red chillies and remove from heat.
4. Gently mix the sautéed mixture along with turmeric powder, lemon juice, green coriander, and coconut with the rice.
5. Serve hot, with plain yoghurt.

1. Boil 3 cups of water in a pot. Add the rice and cook till done. Drain and keep aside.
2. **For the tempering**, heat the oil in a pan; add mustard seeds, asafoetida, curry leaves, green chillies, and ginger. Sauté for 2 minutes. Keep aside.
3. Take a big bowl; mix the rice, yoghurt, and salt.
4. Pour the tempering over the rice mixture and mix.
5. Serve with pickle of your choice.

SERVES 2-4

COOKING TIME

thayir saddham

yoghurt rice

1½ cups / 300 gm / 11 oz	Rice, soaked for 10 minutes
	For the tempering:
2 tbsp / 30 ml / 1 fl oz	Vegetable oil
1 tsp / 3 gm	Mustard seeds (*rai*)
a pinch	Asafoetida (*hing*)
10	Curry leaves (*kadhi patta*)
2 tsp	Green chillies, chopped
2 tsp / 12 gm	Ginger (*adrak*), chopped
3 cups / 600 gm / 22 oz	Yoghurt (*dahi*)
	Salt to taste

Rice, Basmati, soaked for 10 minutes	3 cups / 600 gm / 22 oz
Mangodi (see p. 10)	1 cup / 200 gm / 7 oz
Vegetable oil	1 cup / 200 ml / 7 fl oz
Green cardamom (*choti elaichi*)	5
Black cardamom (*badi elaichi*)	2
Cloves (*laung*)	5
Cinnamon (*dalchini*), 1" sticks	2
Bay leaves (*tej patta*)	2
Cumin (*jeera*) seeds	½ tsp / 1 gm
Salt to taste	
Water	6 cups / 1½ lt / 48 fl oz
Onion, sliced browned	1

mangodi pulao

fried rice with green gram dumplings

SERVES 4-6

COOKING TIME

1. Heat 2 tbsp oil in a wok (*kadhai*); shallow-fry the *mangodi* on medium heat for 2-3 minutes. Remove and drain the excess oil on absorbent kitchen towels and keep aside.
2. Heat the remaining oil in a pan; add green and black cardamom, cloves, cinnamon sticks, bay leaves, and cumin seeds. Sauté on medium heat till the seeds start crackling.
3 Add rice (drained) and *mangodi*. Stir gently, add salt and water.
4. Bring to the boil and then lower heat. Cook until the liquid is absorbed, stirring occasionally, and gently.
5. Serve garnished with browned onion slices.

1. Heat the oil in a pan; add asafoetida and Bengal gram; sauté for 2 minutes.
2. In a large bowl, mix groundnuts, coconut, sesame seeds, green chillies, sugar, and salt together.
3. Mix in the asafoetida mixture and cucumber. Adjust seasoning and serve.

surati salad

crunchy cucumber salad

250 gm / 9 oz	Cucumber (*khira*), small, diced
1 tsp / 5 ml	Vegetable oil
a pinch	Asafoetida (*hing*)
1 tbsp / 25 gm	Bengal gram (*chana dal*), roasted
1 tbsp / 15 gm	Groundnuts (*moongphalli*), roasted, chopped
1 tbsp / 4 gm	Coconut (*nariyal*), fresh, grated
1 tsp / 2 gm	Sesame (*til*) seeds, roasted
2	Green chillies, finely chopped
½ tsp / 1½ gm	Sugar
	Salt to taste

SERVES 2-4

COOKING TIME

Wholewheat flour (*atta*)	2 cups / 200 gm / 7 oz
Fenugreek (*methi*) leaves, chopped	1¾ cups / 50 gm / 1¾ oz
Green coriander (*hara dhaniya*), chopped	1 cup / 25 gm
Green chillies, chopped	2
Salt to taste	
Vegetable oil for shallow frying	

methi ki roti

fenugreek-flavoured unleavened bread

SERVES 2-4

COOKING TIME

1. Mix the wholewheat flour, fenugreek leaves, green coriander, green chillies, and salt together. Add 1 tbsp oil; knead with enough water to make a smooth dough. Cover and keep aside for 15 minutes.
2. Knead again and divide the dough into lemon-sized balls. Roll each out to a 2" diameter disc, smear some oil on the top surface and fold into a half moon. Fold the half moon again into a triangle. Now roll the triangle out.
3. Heat a griddle (*tawa*); lay a triangle flat on it and cook on both sides till tiny brown spots appear. Drizzle a little oil and fry till golden brown on both sides. Remove and repeat till all the triangles are fried.
4. Serve hot with yoghurt and pickle of your choice.

1. Mix all the ingredients together except ghee in a large bowl.
2. Knead the mixture with little water, at a time, into a semi-soft dough.
3. Divide the dough into 15 portions and roll each out to a 4" diameter disc.
4. Heat a griddle (*tawa*); roast the disc evenly on both sides. Now remove the griddle from the heat and roast the disc directly on the flame on both sides till well done but not burnt. Remove and repeat with the other discs.
5. Smear 1 tsp ghee on each disc and serve hot.

SERVES 6

COOKING TIME

missi roti

spicy gram flour bread

2¼ cups / 250 gm / 9 oz	Wholewheat flour (*atta*)
2¼ cups / 250 gm / 9 oz	Gram flour (*besan*)
½ cup / 100 gm / 3½ oz	Yoghurt (*dahi*), hung in a muslin cloth
1 tsp / 2 gm	Carom (*ajwain*) seeds
1 tsp / 2 gm	Red chilli powder
½ tsp / 1 gm	Cumin (*jeera*) seeds
	Salt to taste
2 tbsp / 30 gm / 1 oz	Ghee

Refined flour (*maida*)	3 cups / 300 gm / 11 oz
Vegetable oil	1 tbsp / 15 ml / 1 fl oz
For the filling:	
Green peas (*hara matar*), shelled, ground to a smooth paste	400 gm / 14 oz
Ghee	2-3 tbsp / 30-45 gm / 1-1½ o
Asafoetida (*hing*)	a pinch
Salt to taste	
Sugar	½ tsp / 1½ gm
Soda bicarbonate	a pinch

matar ki puri

shallow fried bread stuffed with green peas

1. **For the filling,** heat the ghee in a pan; add all the ingredients and sauté till the mixture leaves the sides of the pan and is not sticky to touch. Remove and divide the mixture into 15 portions.
2. Rub 1 tbsp oil into the refined flour and knead with enough water into a soft dough. Divide the dough equally into 15 portions.
3. Take a portion of the dough, make a hollow in the centre and fill a portion of the green-pea mixture. Fold over the edges to seal the filling inside. Repeat till all are done. Cover the stuffed balls with a moist cloth and keep aside for 10-15 minutes.
4. With the help of dry flour, roll out each ball into a thin disc of 10" diameter.
5. Roast the disc on a griddle (*tawa*) on both sides using 1½ tsp oil. Remove and repeat with the other discs. Cover with aluminium foil.

SERVES 6

COOKING TIME

1. Sift the wholewheat flour. Rub in the ghee with the fingertips. Knead with enough cold water to make a soft dough.
2. **For the filling,** mix all the ingredients together. Divide the filling into 10 equal portions.
3. Divide the dough equally into 10 portions. Flatten each out into a small disc. Place 1 portion of the filling in the centre, press the edges to seal and reshape into a ball. Roll each ball out to an 8" diameter disc, dusting with dry flour to prevent sticking.
4. Heat a griddle (*tawa*); cook the disc, drizzling 1 tsp ghee, till tiny brown spots appear on both sides. Similarly repeat with the other discs.
5. Serve hot with yoghurt, chutney, and pickle.

SERVES 4

COOKING TIME

aloo paratha

potato stuffed unleavened bread

½ cup / 50 gm / 1¾ oz	Wholewheat flour (*atta*)
1 tbsp / 15 gm	Ghee
	For the filling:
1 cup	Potatoes, boiled, mashed
½ tsp / 1 gm	Garam masala
¾ tsp / 1½ gm	Red chilli powder
1 tsp / 2 gm	Coriander (*dhaniya*) seeds, roasted, powdered
1 tbsp / 4 gm	Green coriander (*hara dhaniya*), chopped
1 tbsp / 12 gm	Onion, chopped
	Salt to taste
	Ghee for shallow frying

Yoghurt (*dahi*), whisked	2½ cups / 500 gm / 1.1 lb
Water	½ cup / 125 ml / 4 fl oz
Salt	1 tsp / 4 gm
Vegetable oil	1 tbsp / 15 ml
Cumin (*jeera*) seeds	1 tsp / 2 gm
Onions, small, chopped	2
Red chilli powder	½ tsp / 1 gm
Turmeric (*haldi*) powder	¼ tsp

pyaz ka raita

yoghurt flavoured with fried onions

SERVES 2-4

COOKING TIME

1. Mix the yoghurt, water, and salt together; keep aside.
2. Heat the oil in a wok (*kadhai*); add cumin seeds and when it starts spluttering, add onions and fry till brown. Add red chilli powder and turmeric powder. Mix and remove from heat.
3. Pour this mixture into the yoghurt mixture and mix well.
4. Smoke (see p. 95) the *raita* with ghee.

1. In a bowl, whisk yoghurt with salt and cumin powder.
2. Add 4 tbsp mint leaves.
3. Refrigerate for half an hour.
4. Sprinkle the remaining mint leaves and serve as an accompaniment to any dish.

pudina raita

mint in yoghurt

3 cups / 600 gm / 22 oz	Yoghurt (*dahi*)
5 tbsp / 20 gm	Mint (*pudina*) leaves, dried, crushed
	Salt to taste
½ tsp / ¾ gm	Cumin (*jeera*) powder

SERVES 2-4

COOKING TIME

..grill boil bake steam stir-fry

allow fry   desserts   deep fry

Almonds (*badaam*), blanched, chopped	500 gm / 1.1 lb
Ghee	1 cup / 200 gm / 7 oz
Milk	1 cup / 200 ml / 7 fl oz
Sugar	3 cups / 450 gm / 1 lb
Green cardamom (*choti elaichi*) powder	1 tsp / 2 gm
Saffron (*kesar*)	a few strands
Silver leaf (*varq*), optional	

badaam halwa

almond delight

1. In a food processor, grind the almonds with a little milk to make a fine paste.
2. Heat the ghee in a heavy-bottomed pan. Add the almond paste and cook on medium heat until light golden.
3. Add the remaining milk and sugar, continue to cook for 10-15 minutes more or till the moisture evaporates and the mixture becomes thick. Remove from heat. Add green cardamom powder and saffron.
4. To serve cold, spread on a greased tray, cut into small squares and decorate with silver leaf. To serve hot, ladle individual portions on to dessert plates and decorate with silver leaf.

SERVES 2-4

COOKING TIME

1. Heat ½ cup ghee in a wok (*kadhai*); add the semolina and sauté on low heat till a pleasant aroma emanates and is golden brown.
2. Add the saffron mixture, water, and sugar. Cook till the water evaporates completely.
3. Add the remaining ghee and sauté till the mixture leaves the side of the wok. Mix in the green cardamom powder.
4. Serve warm garnished with fried raisins and cashew nuts.

SERVES 2-4

COOKING TIME

rawa kesari

semolina garnished with dry fruits

2½ cups / 250 gm / 9 oz	Semolina (*suji*)
1 cup / 200 gm / 7 oz	Ghee
a few strands	Saffron (*kesar*), soaked in lukewarm water
3 cups / 750 m / 24 fl oz	Water
3 cups / 450 gm / 16 oz	Sugar
1 tsp / 2 gm	Green cardamom (*choti elaichi*), powdered
1 cup / 120 gm / 4 oz	Raisins (*kishmish*), fried
50 gm / 1¾ oz	Cashew nuts (*kaju*), fried

Broken wheat (*dalia*)	1 cup / 100 gm / 3½ oz
Ghee	½ cup / 100 gm / 3½ oz
Aniseed (*saunf*)	1 tsp / 1½ gm
Almonds (*badaam*), blanched, halved	8-10
Coconut (*nariyal*), slivers	1 tbsp / 15 gm
Water	2 cups / 500 ml / 16 fl oz
Sugar	½ cup / 75 gm / 2½ oz
Green cardamom (*choti elaichi*), crushed	4

lapsi

sweet porridge with broken wheat

SERVES 4-6

COOKING TIME

1. Heat the ghee in a wok (*kadhai*); add aniseed and sauté till it starts spluttering.
2. Add broken wheat and stir-fry till it is well browned.
3. Add almonds and coconut (keep aside a few for garnishing), and water; bring to the boil. Lower heat and cook till the broken wheat becomes tender.
4. Add sugar and stir till it dissolves completely.
5. Remove from heat and garnish with almonds and coconut.

1. Heat the ghee (for frying) and fry the cottage cheese lightly. Remove and put aside.
2. Heat 2 tbsp ghee in a pot; lightly sauté the almonds, currants, coconut, dates, and black peppercorns for 1 minute.
3. Add water, sugar, and green cardamom. Stir till the mixture comes to the boil. Lower heat and cook for 5 minutes.
4. Soak the saffron in 2 tsp of hot water and crush it with the back of a spoon. Mix into the pot and stir well.
5. Add rock candy and lemon juice; stir again. When the syrup becomes thick (not dry), remove from heat. Serve warm.

SERVES 4

COOKING TIME

shufta

dry fruits in sugar syrup

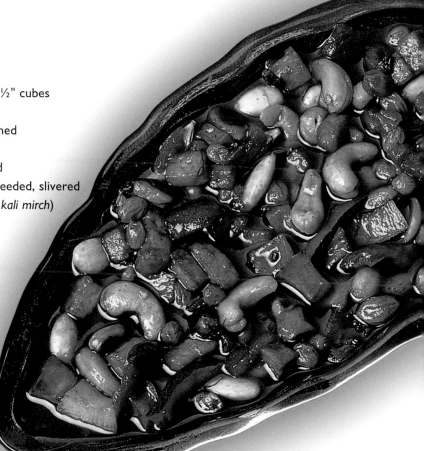

250 gm / 9 oz	Cottage cheese (*paneer*), ½" cubes
	Ghee for frying
½ cup / 60 gm / 2 oz	Almonds (*badaam*), blanched
100 gm / 3½ oz	Currants (*sultanas*)
¼ cup / 25 gm	Coconut (*nariyal*), slivered
1 cup / 50 gm / 1¾ oz	Dried dates (*khajoor*), deseeded, slivered
1 tsp / 6 gm	Black peppercorns (*sabut kali mirch*)
1 cup / 250 ml / 8 fl oz	Water
2 cups / 300 gm / 11 oz	Sugar
6	Green cardamom (*choti elaichi*), crushed
½ tsp	Saffron (*kesar*)
50 gm / 1¾ oz	Rock candy (*mishri*)
1 tbsp / 15 ml	Lemon (*nimbu*) juice

Rice, washed, soaked for 10-15 minutes	2½ cups / 500 gm / 1.1 lb
Water	2 cups / 500 ml / 16 fl oz
Jaggery (*gur*)	1¼ cups / 250 gm / 9 oz
Coconut (*nariyal*), grated	1¼ cups / 150 gm / 5 oz
Ghee	¾ cup / 150 gm / 5 oz
Salt to taste	
Green cardamom (*choti elaichi*), seeds	1 tsp / 2 gm
Banana leaves, cut into 4" squares	4

yel adai

coconut and rice pancakes

SERVES 2-4

COOKING TIME

1. To prepare the jaggery syrup, boil the water, add jaggery and stir well. Remove the scum from time to time. Cook till the syrup is reduced to ¼th.
2. Add the coconut and cook for 5-8 minutes more. Stir in ghee reserving about 1 tbsp.
3. Grind the rice with enough water to make a batter of dropping consistency. Add salt and green cardamom seeds.
4. Smear the remaining ghee over the banana leaves. Place them over hot plates so that the leaves become soft. Pour the rice batter over the banana leaves, spread the jaggery mixture and fold in the shape of an envelope. Steam (see p. 95) for 18-20 minutes. Serve hot or cold.

1. **For the crêpes,** mix all the dry ingredients together in a bowl.
2. Beat the egg with the sugar till foamy. Mix in the milk / half milk and water. Pour this gradually into the flour mixture to prevent lumps from forming. Beat well for 1 minute. Leave to stand for 15 minutes.
3. Grease and heat a 6"-frying pan lightly with ghee; pour 2 tbsp batter into it, tilting to coat the base thinly. Cook covered for a minute. Remove and repeat till all the batter is used up.
4. **For the filling**, in a pan, add the sugar / jaggery syrup and coconut; cook for a few seconds. Remove from heat and cool.
5. Place a little filling on each pancake and roll tightly.
6. Serve on a dish and sprinkle with grated coconut.

SERVES 4-6

COOKING TIME

ale bele

coconut crêpes

For the crêpes:

1¼ cups / 125 gm / 4 oz	Refined flour (*maida*)
a pinch	Baking powder
¼ tsp / 1 gm	Salt
1	Egg
1 tbsp / 20 gm	Granulated sugar
1 cup + 3 tbsp / 240 ml / 8 fl oz	Milk / half milk and half water

For the filling:

3 tbsp / 60 gm / 2 oz	Sugar / grated jaggery (*gur*), dissolved in 1 tbsp water1 on low heat
2 cups / 200 gm / 7 oz	Coconut (*nariyal*), grated
	Ghee for frying

Almonds (*badaam*)	4 cups / 500 gm / 1.1 lb
Sugar	2¾ cups / 400 gm / 14 oz
Water	½ cup / 125 ml / 4 fl oz
Silver leaves (*varq*)	2-3

badaam burfee

almond fudge

SERVES 10

COOKING TIME

1. Soak the almonds in boiling water for 6-7 minutes. Drain, remove the skin and grind to a coarse paste.
2. Heat the sugar and water together in a pan; stir gently till the sugar dissolves completely. Bring the sugar syrup to the boil and then simmer till bubbles start forming.
3. Add the almond paste and cook, stirring constantly, till the mixture leaves the sides of the pan. Remove from heat.
4. Spread the mixture evenly on a greased plate and smoothen the top. Keep aside to cool and decorate with silver leaves.
5. Cut into squares or diamond shapes and serve.

1. Sift the flour and salt together.
2. Beat the eggs with the sugar till thick and foamy. Stir in the milk / coconut milk and vanilla essence and mix well.
3. Add the egg mixture to the flour, gradually, stirring well to make a smooth, thin batter. Leave the batter to rest for 15 minutes.
4. Heat the oil well. Rest the waffle iron (mould) in the hot oil for 2 minutes to heat. Remove and dip immediately into the batter, making sure that the batter coats only the bottom and the sides of the mould and does not go over the top. Transfer immediately to the hot oil. Hold the iron in the oil till the waffle is golden brown and loosens easily. Remove and drain on a plate lined with paper towels. Continue till all the batter is over, heating the mould for a few seconds in the oil before dipping into the batter each time.
5. Cool and store in an airtight container.

SERVES 6-8

COOKING TIME

rose de coco

fried waffles

1¾ cups / 175 gm / 6 oz	Refined flour (*maida*)
¼ tsp / 1 gm	Salt
2	Eggs
3 tbsp / 60 gm / 2 oz	Castor sugar
1½ cups / 300 ml / 11 fl oz	Milk / Coconut milk
½ tsp / 2½ ml	Vanilla essence
	Vegetable oil for deep-frying

glossary

Baste: Moisten the meat, poultry or game with oil / butter during roasting.

Batter: A mixture of flour, liquid and sometimes other ingredients of a thin, creamy consistency.

Blend: To mix thoroughly two or more ingredients.

Broil: Dry roast the food items in a heavy-bottomed pan on low heat without using oil or water.

Coat: To cover food that is to be fried with flour, egg, and breadcrumbs or batter.

Dum: Slow oven or *dum pukht* cooking means cooking on low heat in a vessel with a tightly-fitted lid, which is sometimes sealed with dough or aluminium foil. Heat is applied from above and below the pot so that the food stews slowly in its own juices, and absorbs the delicate flavours of the added spices and herbs.

Grease: To coat the surface of a dish or tin with fat to prevent food from sticking to it.

Grind: To reduce hard food such as pulses, lentils, rice, and so forth, to fine or coarse paste in a grinder or blender.

Julienne: Garnished with fine strips of cooked or raw vegetables.

Knead: To work a dough by hand or machine until smooth.

Marinade: A seasoned mixture of oil, vinegar, lemon juice, and so forth, in which meat, poultry or fish is left for some time to soften and add flavour to it.

Purée: To press food through a fine sieve or blend it in a blender or food processor to a smooth, thick mixture.

Rub in: To incorporate the fat into flour using the fingertips.

Seasoning: Salt, pepper, spices, herbs, and so forth, added to give depth of flavour.

Simmer: To boil gently on low heat.

Skewer: Fasten together pieces of food compactly on a specially designed long pin, for cooking.

Smoking: The process of imparting a smoked flavour to the preparation. Heat a piece of coal over the flame till it becomes red hot. Overlap 2-3 onion peels to form a small cup. Place it in the middle of the dish, with the preparation to be smoked. Place the coal in the onion-peel cup. Smoke with either of the following:

1. Smoking with garlic paste: Put ½ tsp of garlic paste on the coal. Pour 1 tsp ghee on it. Immediately cover with a lid and smoke for 5-7 minutes.
2. Smoking with cloves: Put 3 cloves on the coal. Immediately cover with a lid, smoke for 5-7 minutes.
3. Smoking with ghee: Put 1 tsp ghee on the coal. Immediately cover with a lid and smoke for 5-7 minutes. For best results, this process must be done quickly, so it helps to have everything handy.

Steam: To cook food in steam. Generally food to be steamed is put in a perforated container which is placed above a pan of boiling water. The food should not come into contact with the water.

Syrup: A concentrated solution of sugar in water.

Tandoor: Tandoor is a large coal-fired oven. It is easily adaptable to the oven, the electrical grill or the microwave. Tandoor is akin to the western barbecue, but with more delicate flavours and with marinades which enhance the flavour of the principle ingredient.

Temper: To fry spices and flavourings in hot oil or ghee, and to pour this over the main preparation.

Whip: To beat rapidly and introduce air into an ingredient; usually cream.

Whisk: To beat rapidly to introduce air into a light mixture; usually of egg.

index